My Own Harlem

Second Edition

To Justicia & Brismare,

You both have all the potential in the world.

Continue to Dream;

10-24-98

Published by Addax Publishing Group Inc.
Copyright © 1998 by Pellom McDaniels III
Photography by Gary Carson
Designed by Randy Breeden

For Information address:
Addax Publishing Group, Inc.
8643 Hauser Drive, Suite 235, Lenexa, KS 66215
Revised Second Edition 1998

ISBN: 1-886110-67-0

Printed in the United States of America

Distributed to the trade by Andrews McMeel Publishing
4520 Main Street
Kansas City, MO 64111

1 3 5 7 9 10 8 6 4 2

Preface

The Harlem Renaissance of the early 1920's and 1930's was a time of emerging African American internal and external change. The artistic and literary explosion was an inevitable circumstance of this change. The experiences that were sequestered in the minds of African Americans were to become the fuel of revolution. Today it represents the growth and development of the African American culture in the eyes of their fellow Americans. It was truly a time of personal exploration and freedom of thought and expression.

"My Own Harlem," represents my emergence as an individual with all the influences of upbringing, culture, and community. In this chronicle are writings that express my love of jazz and my thoughts about our history and community. There are also pieces that speak of my family, childhood, and their contribution to my development as an individual.

"My Own Harlem," is an attempt to share with others my thoughts and feelings as I celebrate my own personal renaissance.

6

Contents

*   *Second Edition additional works*

Foreword
by Marcus Allen

Paul Robeson, Langston Hughes, W.E.B. DuBois, were men who through writing, speaking and acting gave the African American community hope and direction, and the world an opportunity to see the beauty and the tragedy of the black experience in America. These men as well as hundreds of others wrote to open the minds and the hearts of their readers as well as their tormentors.

For the past five years I have had the opportunity to work with, and around an individual who, in the same spirit of Robeson, Hughes and DuBois, has dedicated himself to change. He pursued his dream of playing professional football, when all around him said it was impossible. After signing with the Kansas City Chiefs, he did not rest content with this great accomplishment. I, and the rest of our teammates, watched as Pellom wove himself into the fabric of Kansas City. He has, and continues to, make himself available to the people of Kansas City for all manner of charitable activities. He founded the Arts for Smarts Foundation, which acquaints disadvantaged children with the applied and creative arts, and provides funding for art programs in schools and community centers.

It's interesting when you work with someone for a long period of time, you have the chance to see how they handle both disappointment and success. Pellom has always worked hard and never taken his achievements for granted. He reacts to success and failure in the same way: he works harder and prepares to meet the next challenge.

This collection of writings from Pellom McDaniels is more than a book of poetry, it is a metaphor for man who has discovered the flame of conscious thought and endless compassion. In a time of deceptive heroics and selfish pursuits, Pellom uses all that is available to him to ensure the lives of others are complete. Using his hands and his heart he helps those in need.

Well beyond his years in his pursuits he is the embodiment of those heroes that sought change through intellectual thought, and intellectual thinking. I am honored to write this preamble for someone I feel is an agent for change in the world in so many ways.

My beginning

My grandfather, I barely knew.
His memory was washed away,
with the absence of my father.
His identity a mystery
until my adult years.

Now I stand over a grave site
that gives no indication of his ever living,
of my existence,
of our name.

Who was he,
what did he like,
what did he die of?

All of these things a mystery to me.

There was no marker for the grave,
just a number.

1470.

I sit and swell with anger.
He deserves to be known,
to be recognized,
to be.

I am the grandson of 1470 no longer.

He has a name and a past,
the past I have identified,
the past that I have dug up,
and exposed to all.

Pelham N. McDaniel was a man.
Pelham N. McDaniel was me,
and now I am found.

The evolution of jazz

The evolution of jazz
is a story of need.
Need to get high on the Kansas City sound,
need to get higher on bootleg whiskey,
need to get highest on some of Mom's masterpiece marijuana.

The evolution of jazz
is a story of economics.
Who's got the money to give
and how did they get it,
who wants the money
and what are you willing to do for it,
who takes the money
and what are they going to do with it.

The evolution of jazz
is a story of survival.
Survival of a man with no education
and no chance to become rich,
survival of a woman with no husband
and no education,

and no chance to become comfortable.
Survival of a system that made
prostitutes,
pimps,
and junkies
out of the innocent.

The evolution of jazz
is a story of the present.
The present unemployment rate,
the present social problems faced in the black community,
the present condition of the Negro
in the American society.

The evolution of jazz
is ever-evolving.

Evolving in what--I don't know.
Who will win--it's obvious.
Who will pay--that is the question.

A mural painted

Black and white,
it covers the side of a building,
a building in the black district.

The building sits,
waiting for a wrecking ball
or a divine prayer to be answered.

The watcher looks out
across a parking lot on the corner,
it looks at passersby.

People walk,
and sit at the bus stop,
faces unashamed
and dim.

Tears fall from its eyes,
but no one stops.

It can see what has happened
to its physical dream.
It can see the result of forbidden fruit tasted,
and tears fall from its eyes.

It sees the little babies without fathers,
passive mothers using the unconditional being
to fill a void
vacated by the sperm donor.

It sees babies having babies,
with nowhere to turn,
with no light to guide them
from the abyss of judgment.

It sees the mourners
carrying white stakes,
miniature crosses,
to plant in soft,
fertile ground.

This stake is 91,
it is planted next to 90.

Zombies walk up and down
the boulevard
and take comfort on the wall,
smudged with filth and trash.

The surveyors rest
before their next expedition
in search of the fountain of forever.

It sees the parked cars,
that smell of sin in front of him,
his eyes swell with pain.

Martin looks across the parking lot,
to the bus stop.
He sees passersby
with their gold teeth,
he sees them,
with their pretty hair and manicured
fingernails,
as they wait at the bus stop.

He hears them speak:
"Fuck that nigga!
That bitch ain't shit.
Kiss my black ass."

He sheds his tears,
while his people trade
each others' souls
for concrete and asphalt.

While a man turns numbers
on a sign,
keeping count
of the deaths this year.

A billboard reads:

May 2, 1927
Musicians of Greater Kansas City would like to
celebrate National Music Week with the
Annual Musicians Ball.
Astounding Music! Phenomenal Music!
Continuous dancing to the exhilarating tunes
of 8 great bands.
Admission 50 cents.
Dancing will last all night long.
Tonight the one and only Bennie Moten
Orchestra American's Greatest Rhythm Band.

"Time to get the pomade and the grease
ready for the ladies."

"Time to get this horn polished real nice like,
them women like it when the horn's shining
when I'm blowing."

"Time to get some new drumsticks,
these about had it."

19

"Time to go pick up my shoes from the shop,
got a gig tonight and the women love them pretty shoes."

"Time to get my hair did up,
them fine men love a pretty curl job."

"Time to get my razor,
them crazy niggas be out tonight."

My Own Harlem

I got two Victrolas at home
and a hundred records to play
can't seem to find the time to listen.

I got two Victrolas at home
and no music to listen to.
The records are old
and some are scratched.

I got the time to find them record players
but I can't find no music
to listen to.

I can't go to 18th & Vine
'cause it ain't there no more,
   no more,
        no more.

They tore down the spirit a long time ago.
They took the heart
right out of the city
a long time ago
and I can't find no music to play.

I got plenty of records
but they don't say a thing.

I've heard that back in the depression
when the rest of the country was almost at a stop,
ol' 18th & Vine was jumpin'.

When most people couldn't eat,
black folks was livin' alright
and having a good time
down on 18th & Vine.

Nightclubs coming and going
The Sunset
Cherry Blossom and
Club Harlem
gave any town a run for their money.

All that went down
and not a star in the street.
It looks like the depression came back
but, the heart is still missing.

The Paris of the Plains
Sin City,
call it what you please.

My Victrola works pretty good,
but I still don't have any music.

One hundred records
and no Bennie Moten,
Walter Page,
or Count Basie.

Can't find no good music to play
on my Victrola.

One hundred records
and
no
good
music.

Sleep Walkers

Sleeping is for thieves,
 for they steal the energy of life
and all its rewards.

Wasting thoughtless action
and pursuing empty goals
with empty purpose.

Dreaming of what could be,
acting on nothing.

They have no need for beds or cots
for
    they sleep on their feet
    they sleep when they
enunciate
    they sleep when they
ejaculate

They complain about the
weather
    their government
    their lovers
    their situation

But, they continue to sleep.

They sleep even now as they read.

They steal from my precious,
limited, and bountiful resource

Time.

Yeah we had jazz

You can bet it was great
to see the bands
jumpin' off every stage
in the battle of the bands
at almost every club in downtown.

Yeah, we had jazz,

it was hip.
If you played,
you got the finest women
to go home with, the best food
at the best restaurant you could afford
If it was black, of course.

Yeah, we had jazz,

it was swingin'.
Dances almost every night.
Cost 50 cents to get in
and
you could bring your own bottle.

Yeah, we had jazz,

it was a money maker.
If you owned a club
you could make money
from holding dances and contests
even placing side bets on who would win.

Yeah, we had jazz,

it was it was sinful.
You could get anything you wanted downtown
Find a girl for everyday of the week
down on 18th & Vine.
Even The Man was down here
checkin' out the scene on the sly.

Yeah, we had jazz

it was crooked.
All the gangsters sold the booze,
and if you tried
you died.
No time to die,
so most didn't try.

Yeah, we had jazz,

it was good for the time.
When the depression came
it passed right over the Paris of the Plains.
Everybody was making money,
everybody had a hustle that paid off.

Yeah, we had jazz,

that's all we had.
Soon as the depression was over,
and people didn't have to sneak downtown anymore
they started to move away.

And that officer,
who used to go see my sister
he calls me nigger now
like he forgot who I was.

I was the one who let him in the door.
I was the one he gave two dollars
to leave for a couple of hours.

Yeah, we had jazz,

that's all we had.

Parade Park

Flower dresses and bonnets,
dangle in closets,
waiting for a celebration.

Fedoras brushed and
wing tips polished to dazzle
the eye of the beholder,
and boost the ego of the owner.

The good humor man
with a truck full of ice cream
and popsicles,
wishes to park near the fountain
in the summer
to satisfy imaginary customers.

But, the dying have no reason
to celebrate or lead a parade.
They watch the grass grow,
remembering when it was green.

Billie gets a chance

Play them drums boy!

          Rat, ta, tat, arat, ta, tat!

Tear the skin off 'em!

        At, ta, tat, arat, ta, tattat, arat, ta, tat!

Oh yeah, where's the horn at?!
Lemme hear that horn!

        Dunna, dunna, dunn,
    duh, duh, duhhhhhhhhhh, dunna,
          dunna

Oh yeah,
bring it on home Billie!
I can't hear you bring it home!

Oh, what a little moonlight can
do, oh what a little moonlight can do!

Oh Yeah!

Oh! What a little moonlight can
doooooo!

That's what got you here!

Yes sir, Mr. Smith.

I'll see you tomorrow night.

Oh,
make sure you leave
out the back door this time.
Or I'll send your Black Ass
back to New York
in a box.

Yes sir, Mr. Smith.

His place of worship

The gas station closed down
on the corner,
but don't matter
I don't drive anyway.

Long as they don't tear down the temple.

Mrs. Jenkins got robbed last week
and they set the house on fire.
Damn shame.

Long as they leave the temple alone, I'm okay.

Ebinezer Baptist burned down last month
and they say it was electrical.
It was old anyway.

I hope the temple got insurance.
I got to get there after work to tithe
and the nearest one is across town.

Sho' hope nothing happens to that place.

Speak of the devil.
There goes a fire truck down the road.
Please God, don't let that be the temple.

I sho' do love the paint job they did on the outside.
The parking lot looks wonderful too.
They got some iron over the door it looks like.

"Hey, Mr. Franks. How we doin' today?"

"I'm fine Leroy. What may I do for you today?"

"Just came to pay my respects, sir. Been a lot of fire and
accidents lately and it kinda got me worried about you
over here, so I just come to pay may respects."

"Thank you for the hospitality, but come one Leroy, you
didn't walk down here for nothing. What can I do for you?"

"Well, since I'm here, I might as well. Let me have a fifth
of Thunderbird and a cup of ice. I get paid tomorrow, so
can you put it on credit 'til then?"

"I sure can, but you know if you don't pay
tomorrow, the price doubles."

"Yes, sir."

"Plus, I know where you live anyway,
and you ain't going no where soon anyhow,
right?"

"You know it."

East and West on 18th Street

The Sears plant finally closed down
a couple of years back
and the dying neighborhood
almost took its last breath.

Garbage piles up on a vacant lot
on Walrond
right off Highway 70
but it goes unattended.

There's a community college on Prospect
I didn't know until I saw the sign
on a vehicle in the front.

A liquor store sits across the street.
I ask the question why?
Even in the face of prosperity
--hope and education--
the monster still peddles its poison.

Highland had been the scene
of lively times and economic progress
but not for blacks.

The once famous Gem Theater
is now under reconstruction
after years of neglect and decay.

Row houses still line Highland Street.
Their doors hanging off
their hinges.
Windows boarded up
concealing the past.

Flakes of green,
almost lime green paint
cling to the foundation
like most in this area.

The glory days long gone,
never looking at the why
or the how,
or can it happen again.

Will dejavu be the next performance,
or will we be reborn as inventors of the craft?

New brick is being laid,
paint sits in boxes,
stacked on pallets in a warehouse
waiting for a dress rehearsal.

Jack London was here

When I was a kid
I remember reading
The Call of the Wild
and
White Fang,
stories written by Jack London.

He interested me more
than any other author, as a child,
probably because his name
was on so many things around the Bay Area.

I read about his adventures and travels
around the world.
How he would leave for long periods of time
and return with a multitude of stories
and an assortment of adventures.

As a child,
I didn't have to look far for someone
comparable to the personalities
created by the man I read about as a child.

My father is, in fact, the reincarnated urban
version of the world famous author.

His sea consists of street lights
and stop signs.
His waves are sirens and
and the sound of gun fire.

His anchor once again has raised
and his sail has become consumed.

Alaska,
Montana,
the Bering Strait
maybe next time
the letter I'll find in my mailbox
will be from Japan.

Yeah, Jack was here.
When is he coming back?
Not even he knows that.
But, he will.

He always does.

The negative thoughts I can live without

I remember the things that happened.
I have grown from them
not dwelt on them
for their memory to spur my every
breathing moment.

I lived in the house
with the big, white car in the driveway,
and the green house
with the camper parked out front.

I lived the same memories
that you seem to use like glue
to hold the reality of your life together.

Instead of tucking them
neatly in a pillowcase
and laying my head on them
as a security blanket.
I have made them into the stairs of my life,
and I have been climbing for a long time.

Each memory taking me further in life,
and in happiness.
Each having its own significance in my life,
and each with a purpose.

Shake your pillowcase free of those spurs,
or plant them in your garden,
near the rose bushes.

The pain you feel when you think of the past
will be washed away
by the beautiful fragrance.

Life

She dances in the shadow of the moon
with grace of an angel.

Her skin ripe with age,
but smooth as a peach in season.

Only the wise know her origin,
only the foolish ignore her warnings.

Her touch can be magical
to all who are entranced by her beauty,
or deadly to those who plunder her treasure.

A mystery to the eyes of man,
but a cherished thought of untimely spirit.

She is consumed by applause
and curtain calls.

Straight up

Don't ask me what I want to hear
if you ain't got no jazz.

I don't want to hear no watered down Sonny Rollins,
Art Tatum or Charlie Parker.

I'll take mine straight.

Don't give me no generic Miles
or Booty Dizzy.

I'll take it straight up you hear me.

In fact,
give me the whole damn bottle.

I feel like getting high.

Blue

I've heard that the color blue
taste like ambrosia,
smells like jasmine,
feels like silk,
and sings like Lady Day.

I've heard that the color blue
will make you fall in love with life,
give you peace of mind,
open your soul,
and make you embrace all that is.

I've heard that the color blue
gives you heart ache for just a minute
and the pain of it breaking
and then nothing.

I've heard that you love to cry,
you love the taste of salty tears.

I've heard that you look good in Blue.

You like the blues

You say you like the blues.
You like the way it makes you feel,
like the world has forgotten you
and left you to guard for yourself.

You say you like the blues.
You like the sound that the rain makes
on the stained glass windows of your heart,
while Sade sings to you,
while you wipe the tears from your eyes
and contemplate the end of living.

You say you like the blues.
You like the sound of breaking glass,
the lovely percussion of it makes on oak,
while the picture of your lover floats in the toilet,
torn into a million sinking rafts on a tidy sea.

You say you like the blues.

But the blues,
        don't
                care
                        a
                                thing
                                        about
                                                you.

Two shades of blue

As I see it,
there are two shades of blue
in this world.

One that makes us feel good,
and the other that makes us feel
even better.

Jesus Christ in one hand,
BB King in the other.

And here we are,
stuck in between the good book
and the record store.

Paradox

There is a tragedy,
it is unending.

Hide it?
We fail.

We,
and the light of darkness
continue to hold this enigma
like some obscure companion.

Unable to breath without its aid.

Like a metronome,
it keeps our lives moving.
Sometime forward?

Maybe,
it doesn't move at all.

We still dislike what we are.
Children of quintessence.

Picasso's Dream

Misplaced lover
do you think of me when you sleep?
Indulge me.
Look deep into your soul
and you will see me
touch the sanctuary of your inferno.

I have come to take you home
and love you today.
The essence of your being
has called me near.

Misplaced lover,
do you think of me when you bathe.
I know you smell the linens
and imagine my tragedy.

In private you embrace my silhouette.
You wash me.
I will return to fill the vacancy.
Soon.

Oh fantasy of my psyche,
I too,
will love you throughout time.

To my friends

Liu Tsung-yuan closed a poem by saying;
if I could change into a million selves I'd send one to climb each
peak and gaze far off towards home.

I too wish I could divide myself into a million selves
and reach out across the lands
to touch every heart,
every soul,
every hand,
who was in need of comfort
and compassion.

A friend.

If I could do so,
I would spread
the endless compassion
of God.

Friends look towards home,
our father is waiting,
watching.

Professor Washington

A voice, abundant in wisdom, echoes through a theater filled with students whose eyes are directed towards the wise one.

"Throughout the history of the world, the slave has always played a major role in the development of nations. Whether it involved the building of the pyramids, or the building of empires, the African continent and its inhabitants have been subjected to this abuse by not only foreign powers, but also by its own people. Many countries have depended on the slave as a necessity to help drive their economic progress; such was the case of the United States."

The gray haired man pauses to take a drink of water, and inhale the musty air that lingers in the room.

"The early economic progress in the the South can be attributed to the advent of slavery as an institution. The production of surplus products such as cotton, rice, and tobacco were the most important factors in the economic growth of this young country, and in the slave trade."

In the audience whispers begin to erupt and a young man raises his hand.

"Yes, Mr. Thomas," the professor asks.

"Professor Washington, are you saying that the economic growth of the world, in all its success, originated here in the United States?"

Impressed by the inquiry of the students, the smiling Professor Washington responds.

"Correct, Mr. Thomas. Without slavery the economy of the United States and the world would be very different. Economically speaking, without slavery, would consumer demand have been met if the product could not be harvested? Another question, regardless of race, if slavery were illegal and all men were treated as such, where would we be? Can anyone answer that question?"

The professor scans the room for an answer. A hand goes up in the middle of the theater.

"Yes, Miss Johnson."

"Professor, are you condoning the institution of slavery?"

The classroom stirs with murmurs and questions.

"Are you saying that it was necessary that blacks became slaves?"

"On the contrary, Miss Johnson," answers Professor Washington. "It was necessary that a labor force be implemented to allow for capitalism to take place. As you know, the only way to have a capitalistic economy is to have a democratic society, where people can voice their opinions of what they think is right and wrong. Most people are afraid of things they do not know about, and are ready to destroy those things rather than learn about them."

Before a response can filter through the tension, created by the discussion, the bell rings. The loud, clanging noise fills the air and stirs the auditorium. As the students slowly file out of the theater, the professor makes an announcement.

"Don't forget, tomorrow there will be a test on Chapter 21: The triangular trade and the Spanish."

As Professor Washington is gathering his notes together, Mr. Thomas approaches the front table. The table is a pulpit of sorts, where the professor makes his presentations.

"Yes, Mr. Thomas," says the professor, looking up, "may I help you?"

"Yes sir. I've started working on my thesis project, and I was wondering if I could ask you a few questions about the modern black revolution and why it was unsuccessful."

"It's obvious, Mr. Thomas. We don't yet know how to work as a people. You see, even in Africa, we fought against one another for dominance, as animals do for territory. When they brought us to the United States, we were treated like animals and were domesticated for the purpose for which the colonists needed us. Our families were developed with the intention that they would work as laborers. We adapted to the hostile environment, by teaching our children to talk, dress, and react as slaves."

The young man's face becomes twisted and confused.

"Are you saying we are animals? That black people are animals that have been systematically bred for the purpose of work?"

"That is correct. Just as the dog was bred for the purpose of protecting the home, and the herding of cattle and sheep. As the horse was bred for riding and the cow for milking. Africans were broken down, just the same."

"Professor, I have to disagree. These people, the Africans, were forced onto ships that were human cargo carriers, and beaten into submission. They were survivors, not animals."

"Do I look like an idiot, Mr. Thomas? I have studied everything that you think you know, long before you were born. Have you looked at the subject objectively? Tell me something, do you know anything about the Holocaust?"

"Yes."

"What did Hitler do to the Jewish people?

"He tried to exterminate them from Germany--from the world."

"Now, how did he go about doing this?"

"He convinced the German people that the Jews were good-for-nothing people, and compared them to rats."

"How did he accomplish this?"

"Through propaganda?"

"Correct. He dehumanized the entire race by using propaganda to take their faces from them. By making them faceless, it made it easy for German people to blame the Jews for the depression that was taking place in Germany at the time, and the lack of food and terrible economy. Hitler made it easy to gather all the Germans together for a common cause, which was the extermination of an entire group of people."

The wise one pauses to ask his pupil a question.

"What is the topic of your paper, Mr. Thomas?"

"It's the origin of slavery and its international importance to the development of the United States' economy."

"That sounds a little complex and wide open to write about. What you need to do is write about what you know. It tends to hold your interest a lot longer. Learn about why we, as a people, were vulnerable to becoming slaves. Look to Africa, Mr. Thomas."

The young man gives the professor an odd, confused look.

"Why Africa?"

"What wild dog do you see on the Serengeti?"

"The hyena."

"Correct. What is the purpose of the hyena, in the canine family?"

"Purpose? What do you mean, purpose?"

"Everything living has a purpose, Mr. Thomas. The hyena is a scavenger. It travels in a pack and cleans up after the big cats have had their fill. Have you every watched public television and seen the mighty lion stalk a zebra, bring it down, and feed? After which two, maybe three hyena take a chance to grab a couple of scraps for their own dinner, or wait until the lion has had enough, and feed on the carcass?"

"I see what you're saying. It's kind of like our existence here as slaves, always getting the leftovers from the master--pig guts, beef tounge, pig's feet, even hand-me-down clothes. We have set a standard like the hyena."

"Exactly. But, there is just one more thing. If those hyena get together in a pack or clan, they too can bring down their own zebra, and defend it from the lion. In some cases, they can defeat and kill the lion. When they work together, they can defeat any enemy, any time. The problem with the hyena, is that it is so independent and vicious, that it will kill its own for a small piece of meat, or even kill one of its own and eat it."

"Cannibalism?"

"Cannibalism. Until we find out what our purpose is on this continent, in this world, and in our own lives, we will be satisfied with the scraps that are given to us. Good day, Mr. Thomas."

The old scholar grabs his hat and coat, turns on his heel, and proceed to the door of the theater. Before his exit, he turns once again to his pupil.

"Mr. Thomas, there is a lot of information written in books that line the shelves of our library, and a multitude in my office. Feel free to stop by, anytime."

"Yes sir, thank you sir."

"And Mr. Thomas, chapter twenty-one, study it well. I expect and A-plus from you."

With a twinkle in his eye, he opens the door and walks out, closing the door gently behind him.

Tunk
a play in two acts

Characters in Play

Thomas Man in 50s, brother of Loretta
Married to Doris.

Doris Wife of Thomas
A heavy-set woman with a light
complexion. She has an awful
temper, and will say anything that
comes to mind, regardless of the
feelings of others.

Loretta Sister of Thomas. Wife of William.
Mother of Richard and Lonzo.
The matriarch of the family. She
is also the peacemaker of the family.

William Husband of Loretta.
Father of Richard and Lonzo.

Richard Son of Loretta and William, 35 years old
A muscular man who can't keep a steady job
and lives with Loretta, William and Lonzo.
Willing to do most anything for a small
price.

Lonzo Son of Loretta and William, 16 years old.
Quiet, displaced amongst the adults.

John Brother of William
Unfaithful husband having an affair with
Miss Daisey.

Gloria Alcoholic wife of John
Married to John for 12 years. They have
two children. A fiery Mexican woman
who could cook with the women and eat
with the men.

Miss Daisey Elderly girlfriend of John, 65 years old
Lives in the neighborhood with Loretta,
William, and Lonzo. Has a reputation of
being a "sugar mama." She has affairs,
both brief and ongoing, with younger men.
In return, she'll give them money.Tunk

Act I

Setting: *A dining room in the home of Loretta and William with a knitted cloth on the table to protect from scratches. The living is adjacent to the dining room. The living room furniture is nice, but is covered by plastic to protect from wear. The walls of the living room are covered with wallpaper and pictures of relatives, Martin Luther King, Jr., and Jesus. A man with a smoker's voice begins talking.*

Thomas: *Looks at the cards in his hands.* Lonzo! Lonzo! Boy, go to the store and get me some beer! *Looks over his shoulder to the couch where the youthful boy sits watching television.* Can you buy beer? Are you old enough? How old are you anyway?

Lonzo: *Answers in a shy voice.* I'm sixteen.

Thomas: *Turns all the way around to look at Lonzo on the couch.* Sixteen?!! Boy, I thought you was twenty-one by now! *Pauses.* You can still buy beer. *Looks at his cards.* I used to drink it when I was ten, and buy it when I was twelve. So, I know you can go get a couple of cans.

Doris: Thomas! *Yells in a crabby, annoying voice.* You know damn well that boy can't buy no damn beer, with your dumb ass! Doris is a heavy set woman, with a yellow complexion, and an awful temper.

William: He can buy beer. *Pulls his cards away from his face, but still studying them intently.* Just send a note with him, with the telephone number on it, in case they want to call and to see who it's for.

Loretta: *Comes in from the kitchen.* Don't send that boy to no store to buy no damn beer. Ya'll need to get up off your lazy behinds and go yourself – or send Richard!

Richard: *Sits up suddenly with excitement in his eyes.* I'll go to the store if you buy me a bottle of MD 20/20. *Richard is a muscular man who can keep a steady job and lives with Loretta, William, and Lonzo. He is always willing to do something, for a small price.*

William: *With a look of disgust on his face.* MD 20/20?! You's a sick-ass nigga. That's some terrible shit you know. I'd hate to see your kidneys.

Loretta: *Growling.* Lonzo, call your Uncle John on the phone and tell him to bring some beer when he comes.

Lonzo gets up off the couch slowly.

Loretta: *Angry.* Boy! Get in that kitchen like I said and call that man!

Thomas: *With a harsh, patronizing laugh.* Tell him to bring two of whatever. That alcoholic will drink it all his self. *Pauses to look at Richard, shaking his head.* Between John and Rich, they couldn't donate nothin' to nobody!

Doris: *Speaks wrathfully, while pulling card from the deck.* That's another no good nigga, no good to the bone.

William: *Chimes in, pointing directly at Doris.* Watch your mouth woman! That's my brother you're talkin' about! What you say about him, you say about me!

Doris: *Laughing out loud.* I know!

The table breaks into laughter.

Loretta: *Looks at her cards, remarks softly, almost to herself.* I hope John don't bring that drunk ass Mexican over here.

Lonzo: *Shouts from the kitchen.* Mama, ain't nobody answering the phone over there! *Lonzo had only let the phone ring twice before he hung up. He was hoping they would forget about the beer and just play cards.*

Loretta: *Sternly.* Call Miss Daisey's he might be over there gettin' a little! *She looks across the table at William. She knows that was the wrong thing to say in front of company.*

Lonzo: *With a slight attitude, leaning on the wall at the entrance to the kitchen.* Where's the number at?

Loretta: *Responds quickly.* Look up on top of the refrigerator – in the address book.

Richard: *Looks at his hand, knowing he can't win.* Give me some money and I'll go to the store. *He looks around the table for the first taker of his offer.*

Thomas: *He is the first to reach into his pocket. Sighs.* Here go twenty dollars. Bring me back some pork rinds too. *Looks at Richard, knowing he won't get all of his change back.* And some peanuts.

Richard: *With a stupid grin on his face.* With a twenty, you know I'ma get me a bottle too. *As he stuffs the bills into the pocket of his worn out blue jeans.*

William: *Looks at his cards with a confused look.* A bottle of what?

Loretta: *Looks at William like he's stupid, and mimics him sarcastically.* A bottle of what? None of your damn business! *She reaches back to scratch her behind.*

Richard: *Happy to finally be getting something to drink.* Lonzo, is there any Kool Aid left in the refrigerator?

Lonzo: *Pouring the last of the Kool Aid into a cup, he yells back into the dining room.* Nope, I just drank the rest.

William: *To Richard.* Hell, you might as well stop by the gas station and pay that man a dollar to pump a gallon of regular in your mouth.

Thomas: *Without looking up from his hand, says nonchalantly to William.* Hey man, give the boy some money to get some Gin or Bourbon from the store, with your cheap ass.

William: *Laughs out loud.* Well, I guess you just want to get shitty tonight.

Thomas: *Winking at William, while still keeping an eye on his hand.* I ain't got to drive, so why not!

Doris: *Rolling her eyes from her cards, to look at Thomas.* Don't fool yourself, nigga. *In her deepest, sarcastic voice.* You'll be sleeping with your brother-in-law tonight. *She and Loretta laugh out loud.*

Thomas: *Looks at Doris with a serious gaze.* What the hell you talkin' bout. I betchu I'll be home in the bed by 2 o'clock.

Loretta: *Grinning broadly, with a chuckle in her voice.* Doris, remember last time they got drunk? *Trying to hold back laughter.* One was sleeping with his mouth open, and the other peed in the bed like a baby and he didn't even know it! *Laughing out loud with tears in*

69

her eyes. I was hoping a damn roach would've crawled in his mouth and choked him!

Doris: *Also in tears from laughing.* I remember, *pauses to wipe her face.* 'cause I had to drive home with him smelling like a pair of pissy draws!

Both Doris and Loretta crack up at the table.

Thomas: *Upset, places his hand down on the table.* Why is it, almost yelling, that anytime we get together with other folks you gotta bring that up?! *Picks his hand back up and mumbles.* Maybe I will sleep here tonight. Better than going home with your fat ass! *Huffing.*

Loretta: *After pausing to catch her breath.* The hell you will!

William: *Hesitates and stammers.* I pay the bills in this house, woman. You don't run a damn thing. *Looks at Thomas.* He is my guest!

Loretta: *Raises her voice to suppress her laughter.* Let him sleep in the bed with you. *Beginning to chuckle.* He might get a little more action than I get!

Loretta and Doris burst into laughter again.

Thomas: *Slams his cards down on the table.* TUNK! Ya'll gots to give the money up!

Everyone looks down at the table to see what he's got.

William: *Frustrated.* Something told me to me to go down last time around.

Everyone throws down their cards. Thomas collects his winnings, leaving a dollar for the next hand.

Thomas: Go on ahead, and deal 'em up!

The set fades to darkness with the sound of cards being shuffled and voices talking over one another.

Act 2

It's 10 PM. Richard is back from the store and everyone has something to drink. Thomas is eating his bag of pork rinds. Doris is smoking a cigarette. Loretta is in the kitchen frying chicken. William is beginning to get drunk and Lonzo is still watching television. The doorbell rings and everyone looks at each other. Loretta looks over at Lonzo, who gets up to answer the door. He opens the door and his Uncle John walks in.

John: *Grins, showing off the gold tooth in his mouth.* Hey boy, whatcha know good?! *He walks in through the open screen door, into the dining room, holding hands with his date.*

Lonzo: *Surprised.* Hey Uncle John. *Tries to suppress laughter.*

Miss Daisey: *Looks at Lonzo, and speaks in a frail, pitiful voice.* You can't speak to nobody boy?

Lonzo looks surprised at her comment.

Miss Daisey: *Looks around at the group.* He acts like that's the only nigga he sees.

Lonzo: *Laughs to himself.* Yes'm, how are you doing? *Lonzo smiles because even he knows about freaky ol' Miss Daisey.*

Miss Daisey: *Turns and spits behind her as she walks in the door.* This muthafucker here trying to get me drunk tonight so he can take advantage of my maturity. *Stammers into the living room.* Probably wants some money or something. *Sucks her teeth, looking at John.* He might just get it, if he treats me right.

Loretta: *Sharply, to John.* What the hell you doing with that woman in my house! You know damn well Gloria gonna come by looking for you over here!

Doris: *Whispers into Thomas' ear.* Loretta about to get in Daisey's behind!

William: *Stands at attention, looking just as surprised as everyone else, but tries to have a little more class.* Hey Daisey, want a beer?

Richard: *Turns to look at his uncle, slurs his words.* Hey Uncle John. I just saw Gloria at the store. I told her you was coming by. *Turns back to the table with a grin on his face.*

John: *Looks like he's seen a ghost.* She was where? *Drops Daisey's hand.* When did you see her?

Richard: *Leans back in his chair and sucks his teeth.* Just about a half-hour ago. *Looks back at the cards in his hand.* She said she was going to be by in a little bit, and to save her a beer.

Loretta: *Wipes her hands with a cup towel and smiles. Looks at John with both her hands on her hips.* You better get out of here with that shit. I don't need ya'll tearing up my house tonight, fightin'.

Doris: *Rolls her eyes up in her head and looks at Loretta.* Let's go to the store, Loretta. I need some more cigarettes.

William: *Stands up, shouting.* Hell no you won't! I know what you up to. *Walks over to Doris, pointing his finger in her face.* Don't start no shit in my house.

Loretta: *Walks over to John and Daisey.* Ya'll need to leave cause I don't want no trouble here tonight. *Walks to the door.* Come on back later on, John, after you take Daisey home.

John: *Looks past Loretta into the open doorway. His eyes look like they are about to pop out of his head.* What are you doing here?

Gloria is standing on the other side of the screen door with a pistol in her hand.

Gloria: *Shouts, shakes the pistol in the direction of John and Daisey.* Get your black ass our here, right now, John. And bring your whore with you! *Pulls on the locked screen door, trying to open it.*

Thomas: *Standing, eyes wide.* Lonzo, go back to your room and call the police before something happens.

Lonzo, just as shocked as everyone remains on the couch looking at the scene in the doorway.

Thomas: *Walks over to the door.* Hey Glo.

Gloria: *Startled by the gesture.* Thomas, what the hell do you want?! *Looks at John with burning eyes, then looks back at Thomas.* You getting a piece of this whore too?! *Gestures at Daisey with the pistol.*

Daisey: *Lunges towards the door.* I got your whore, you greasy wetback! I'll kick off in your ass!

Thomas grabs Daisey and wrestles her back from the door.

Daisey: *Struggling.* Let me go, dammit!

Loretta: *Moves slowly toward Gloria.* Gloria, give me that gun, girl, before you shoot him and go to jail. *Reaches her hand out slowly to take the black peacemaker from Gloria's hands.* Gimme that gun girl.

Gloria: *Tries to hold back tears, heaving and wavering.* He's wrong, Loretta. He ain't nothing but a goddamn dog. *Waves the gun at John again.* He needs to be shot.

Loretta: *Cupping the gun with both hands and taking it from her.* Probably so, but let someone else do it. *Hugs Gloria and leads her into the house.*

John: *Looks at Gloria, puffing out his chest.* Woman, if you ever–

Doris: *Chimes in sarcastically.* What?! Punk me again with your punk ass, John! You thought you was dead! Probably peed on yourself, too! *Laughs out loud.*

Thomas: *Embarrassed by Doris' frankness.* Cool it Doris, and mind your business. *Reaches for one of Doris' cigarettes.*

Doris: *Angry at Thomas' command.* Nigga, don't tell me what to do. *Raises her voice.* You know who runs this show.

Gloria: *Sitting on the couch with Loretta.* You should'a let me shoot his ass and put him out of his misery. *Wipes tears from her eyes.*

Loretta: *Hugs Gloria and consoles her.* It's okay, girl. He ain't worth it. *Looks up at John and Daisey, about to leave the house.* He ain't worth a damn!! *She shouts, so everyone else in the house can hear her.*

Gloria: *Cries and sobs.* You just gonna leave with her, ain't you?! *Fights to stand up.* You don't love me no more? *Walks over to John.* What about our kids? They need a daddy and I need my husband.

Loretta: *Stands next to Gloria.* Girl, you don't need that dog. He ain't no good. *Looks at John and Daisey.* Get the hell out of my house.

William: *Still sitting at the dining room table.* Mind your business, woman. Ain't nobody ask you nothing in the first place. *Looks down at his cards.* Sit your ass down anyhow.

Gloria: *Crying and reaching for John.* What happened to us? What happened to you?

John looks pitiful and embarrassed at his behavior.

Gloria: You still love me don't you?

John: *In a low, solemn voice.* You know I do.

Gloria: Then why? *Pleading.* Why do you do the things you do, to hurt me and the kids? *Takes John's hands.* Come home John. *Reaches around his waist. John embraces her.* Come home with me.

Daisey: *Drunk and unaffected by the scene. Has been released by Thomas and makes her way to the couch. She sits down next to Lonzo, who is watching the scene in the doorway.* I need something to drink. *Looks at Lonzo.* Boy, you sure done grown up fine. How old are you? Twenty-five?

Lonzo looks at the old woman, smiles, shakes his head and turns to watch television.

Richard: TUNK!!

William: You cheatin' nigga! You betta lay off that funny shit. You done forgot who you messin' with.

The lights fade to black.

About the Author

In this version of *My Own Harlem*, as in the first edition, Pellom McDaniels, in Langston Hughes-like-pensiveness, gives us an opportunity to look into the heart of a displaced young man trying to reach out to the world around him. In fearless style, he writes about the development of an African American original, Jazz, and the historic 18th & Vine district of Kansas City.

My Own Harlem, also serves as a vehicle of self renaissance for this enigmatic individual, well beyond his years. This revised version also includes a series of new works entitled, *Two Shades of Blue*.

McDaniels established the "Arts for Smarts" foundation, a program designed to expose disadvantaged children to the fine and applied arts with the goal to encourage both expressive development and creative thinking. In 1998 the Presidents Committee for the Arts and Humanities headed by Harriet Fulbright, recognized "Arts for Smarts" as a national model for community based programs in the United States.

Pellom is a gifted athlete and plays on the defensive line of the Kansas City Chiefs.